Pakistan
& Bangladesh
in pictures

Prepared by Jon A. Teta

VISUAL
GEOGRAPHY
SERIES

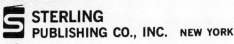

STERLING
PUBLISHING CO., INC. NEW YORK

Oak Tree Press Co., Ltd.
London & Sydney

A new "miracle" rice will help solve Pakistan's food problems.

VISUAL GEOGRAPHY SERIES

Afghanistan	Italy
Alaska	Jamaica
Argentina	Japan
Australia	Kenya
Austria	Korea
Belgium and Luxembourg	Kuwait
Berlin—East and West	Lebanon
Brazil	Liberia
Bulgaria	Malawi
Canada	Malaysia and Singapore
The Caribbean (English-	Mexico
Speaking Islands)	Morocco
Ceylon (Sri Lanka)	Nepal
Chile	New Zealand
China	Norway
Colombia	Pakistan and Bangladesh
Cuba	Panama and the Canal
Czechoslovakia	Zone
Denmark	Peru
Ecuador	The Philippines
Egypt	Poland
England	Portugal
Ethiopia	Puerto Rico
Fiji	Rhodesia
Finland	Rumania
France	Russia
French Canada	Saudi Arabia
Ghana	Scotland
Greece	South Africa
Greenland	Spain
Guatemala	Surinam
Hawaii	Sweden
Holland	Switzerland
Honduras	Tahiti and the
Hong Kong	French Islands of
Hungary	the Pacific
Iceland	Taiwan
India	Tanzania
Indonesia	Thailand
Iran	Tunisia
Iraq	Turkey
Ireland	Venezuela
Islands of the	Wales
Mediterranean	West Germany
Israel	Yugoslavia

PICTURE CREDITS

The publishers wish to thank the following for the use of photographs in this book: Agency for International Development, Washington; APDA Public Relations; Caltex International; Department of Films and Publications, Government of Pakistan; Department of Tourism, Government of Pakistan; Embassy of Pakistan, Washington; Intercontinental Hotels, New York; Pakistan International Airlines; Press Information Department, Government of Pakistan; Carl Purcell; U.S. Department of Agriculture, Washington; World Bank Group, Wash.

Modern facilities at universities and technical schools help prepare a new generation of technicians for Pakistan's future. Here is part of the Punjab University at Lahore.

CONTENTS

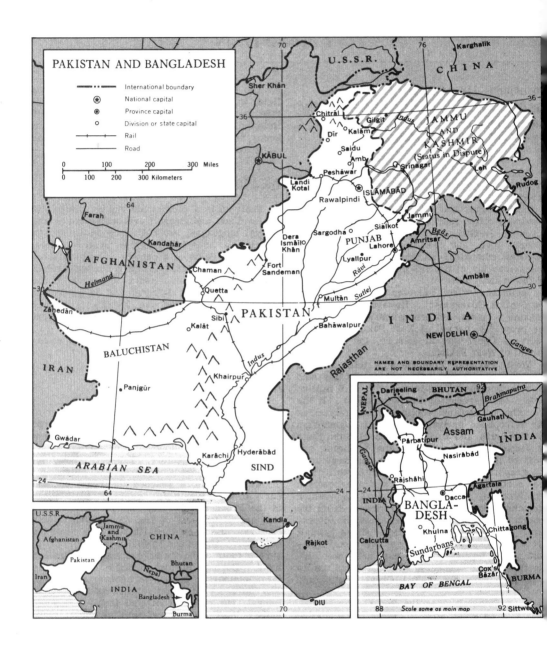

PAKISTAN AND BANGLADESH

—·—·—	International boundary
⊛	National capital
⊙	Province capital
○	Division or state capital
—+—+—	Rail
———	Road

0 100 200 300 Miles

0 100 200 300 Kilometers

U.S.S.R.

CHINA

Karghalik

Sher Khân

Chitrâl

Gilgit

Indus

JAMMU AND KASHMIR (Status in Dispute)

36

Dîr

Kalâm

KÂBUL

Saidu

Ambi

Srinagar

Leh

Rudog

Peshâwar

Landi Kotal

ISLÂMÂBÂD

Jammu

Rawalpindi

Siâlkot

Beâs

Farah

64

Sargodha

PUNJAB

Lahore

Amritsar

Kandahâr

Dera Ismâîlo Khân

Râvi

AFGHANISTAN

Chaman

Fort Sandeman

Lyallpur

Ambâla

Helmand

Quetta

Multân

Sutlej

30

Zâhedân

Sibi

PAKISTAN

Bahâwalpur

INDIA

Kalât

Rajasthan

NEW DELHI

Ganges

BALUCHISTAN

Khairpur

Indus

NAMES AND BOUNDARY REPRESENTATION ARE NOT NECESSARILY AUTHORITATIVE

IRAN

Panjgûr

NEPAL

Darjeeling

BHUTAN

Brahmaputra

Gauhati

Gwâdar

Karâchi

Hyderâbâd

Assam

Pârbatipur

Nasirâbâd

INDIA

ARABIAN SEA

SIND

24

64

Ganges

Râjshâhi

Agartala

24

INDIA

Dacca

BANGLA-DESH

Kandla

Khulna

Chittagong

Sundarbans

Calcutta

Râjkot

Cox's Bâzâr

BURMA

U.S.S.R.

Jammu and Kashmir

CHINA

BAY OF BENGAL

Sittwe

Afghanistan

Pakistan

Bhutan

Nepal

Iran

INDIA

Bangladesh

Burma

DIU

70

88

Scale some os main map

92

Built in 1671 by Aurangzeb, the last of the Mogul emperors, Badshahi Mosque in Lahore is the world's largest Moslem place of worship, with a capacity of close to 100,000 in the vast courtyard where services are held. The Mosque is distinguished by three gleaming white marble domes and a bevy of minarets.

INTRODUCTION

PRIOR TO 1947, there was no Pakistan. It existed only in the dreams of the Moslems who lived in India. Vastly outnumbered and dominated by some 300,000,000 Hindus, the Moslems envisioned a nation of their own in which they could nourish and develop their own political and commercial ambitions, their own religion and culture.

When the British gave independence to India, the brightest jewel in their imperial crown, two areas of the subcontinent where Moslems outnumbered Hindus formed a new nation, Pakistan, as a Dominion within the British Commonwealth.

It was not an easy birth. The new nation came into being amidst great confusion, rioting, and death. The odds seemed against its ultimate survival. The two provinces contained some of the least developed areas of the subcontinent and the thousand miles of Indian territory that divided them was anything but conducive to national unity.

But the Pakistanis found their greatest strength, their fiercest tie, in the very reason for the new nation's existence—their devotion to Islam. The cry of "Pakistan Zindabad" (Long Live Pakistan) was heard throughout the land. The spirit behind that cry has taken the

5

In the fight against cholera, United States health and sanitation advisers have inoculated hundreds of thousands of Pakistanis by the hypospray method.

Pakistanis over seemingly insurmountable obstacles and through the most trying circumstances. Their Islamic nationalism expressed itself anew in 1956, when Pakistan threw off Dominion status, and declared itself an Islamic Republic within the Commonwealth.

In the two decades of its existence, the infant nation has made satisfactory progress in developing its relatively backward economy. A substantial amount of industrialization has taken place, with the help of financial and technical aid from many nations. In the sphere of international affairs, it has earned a reputation for liberal and democratic policies.

The two-part nation has had to cope with a number of critical problems—widespread poverty, unemployment, illiteracy, an exploding population, and an onrushing food shortage.

By 1971, the two parts seemed headed for separation. Widespread clashes between East Pakistanis and government troops (mainly West Pakistanis) led to the death of many civilians and caused a stream of refugees to pour into India.

Then, in December, 1971, India invaded East Pakistan, as the Bengalis rose in rebellion. The Pakistani army was defeated in a matter of weeks and the independent republic of Bangladesh was proclaimed, with Sheikh Mujibar Rahman as its Prime Minister.

Even beasts of burden have to rest sometimes. These camels enjoy the balmy breeze as their masters escape the searing heat of the day at Clifton Beach, a few miles from Karachi on the Arabian Sea.

I. THE LAND

UNTIL 1972, Pakistan was the most populous Moslem state after Indonesia and the sixth most populous nation in the world. Geographically, it consisted of two provinces, East Pakistan (now the independent nation of Bangladesh) and West Pakistan, separated by the expanse of India, a thousand miles apart by land and three times as far by sea. The two provinces differed greatly from each other in language, race, customs, and tradition. Including both regions, Pakistan had an area of 365,529 square miles—roughly equivalent to one-tenth the area of the United States, or about three times that of the British Isles.

Pakistan, with an area of 310,403 square miles, is much larger than Bangladesh. It is bounded by the Arabian Sea on the south, by Iran on the west, Afghanistan on the north and northwest, the disputed state of Kashmir on the northeast and India on the east. It is divided into 13 administrative units, formed from the former Indian provinces of Baluchistan, Sind, the North West Frontier Province, and part of the Punjab. There are also a number of formerly semi-independent small princely states whose rulers have no real power, that acceded to Pakistan.

Snow-capped mountains, fertile valleys and rushing torrents make Gabral, Pakistan, an enchanting place for lovers of natural beauty.

TOPOGRAPHY

The Republic of Pakistan has three main natural regions—the rich agricultural area of the Indus Valley; the dry, unproductive central plain, much of which is sandy desert, that extends southward to the Arabian Sea, an area as inhospitable to life as California's Death Valley; and the sunbaked mountain wall, rent by huge gorges, along the northern, north-western, and northeastern frontiers. The mountain ranges include Nanga Parbat (26,660 feet), between Rawalpindi and Gilgit, the sixth highest mountain in the world; the Hindu Kush Range in the west with Tirich Mir (25,263 feet) the tallest; Mount K2 (Godwin Austen) in the north, the second highest in the world (28,250 feet).

Workers maintain dykes of the Ganges-Kobadak canal near the village of Bheramara. A network of irrigation, drainage, and flood control canals is under construction by the government of Bangladesh in the Kushtia district.

Bangladesh, comprising a total land area of 55,126 square miles, faces the Bay of Bengal on the south and, except for a small strip in the southeast adjoining Burma, is surrounded on three sides by India. It comprises four administrative divisions formed from East Bengal, the Sylhet District of Assam, and the Chittagong Hill Tracts. Topographically, most of

At the Khyber Pass, in the foothills of the Suleman Mountains, a modern highway presents the driver with a maze of hairpin turns.

9

A "goena" (river boat) lies becalmed on the broad waters of the Meghna River in Bangladesh, as the sun begins to rise.

Bangladesh is as flat as a pancake with hardly a hillock visible for miles, except for the northern and eastern borders which are hilly. Only slightly above sea level, most of it is a fertile, water-logged region, with much of the land either delta, marshy wilderness or dense, tropical forest.

WATERWAYS

Five main rivers run through Pakistan: from their sources in the lofty Himalayas, the Indus, Jhelum, Chenab, Ravi, and Sutlej

With the temperature at 110 degrees in the shade, the inhabitants of a small village in the Matlab Bazaar area of Bangladesh protect themselves from the broiling afternoon sun with wide umbrellas. The dwelling on the left and the fence on the right are constructed of bamboo which is plentiful in this region.

Bengalis call this popular old paddle-wheel steamboat the Rocket because it goes so fast. Actually it takes the steamer over 19 hours to beat its stately way from Narayanganj, near Dacca, to the industrial town of Khulna. The same trip can be made by air in less than 30 minutes.

Rivers eventually all join to form the great delta of the Indus River, entering the sea south of Karachi. Without these mighty rivers, Pakistan would revert to desert.

The Indus Basin, lying mostly in Pakistan and partly in India, is the largest canal-irrigated area in the world. Over 60 per cent of the total land under cultivation in Pakistan depends on the vast system of irrigation canals fed by the Indus and its tributaries.

Much of the coast of East Pakistan lies in the enormous delta of the Ganges-Brahmaputra river system. Like the Indus, the Ganges, one of the world's great rivers, also has its source in the melting snows of the Himalayas, flowing east through India. In some areas of Bangladesh, the Ganges measures 10 miles wide. Another great river, the Brahmaputra, which flows south into India and Bangladesh from Tibet,

joins the Ganges before it empties into the Bay of Bengal. The many branches and tributaries of these two mighty rivers criss-cross the entire province—depositing vast quantities of fertilizing silt over the surface of the land, providing an inexhaustible supply of fish, and furnishing the population with a cheap means of transportation.

CLIMATE

The pleasantest months in both countries are November through March, the season that the people refer to as "Eternal Spring." The average temperature in the lowlands during these months ranges from 50° F. to 70° F., with brisk, cool evenings. Since most homes in Bangladesh are not heated, people tend to spend as much time as possible out in the sun

Subsistence farming is the rule for 90 per cent of the population of the semi-arid region of Baluchistan. In an effort to wrest a living from the parched land, the farmers must contend with wretched conditions and crude equipment unchanged since Biblical times.

in winter. Summer—mid-April to mid-June—is considerably hotter with the thermometer often hitting 110 and above. The invigorating sea breezes that refresh coastal Karachi most of the year turn hot and dusty in the summer. A familiar sight in Hyderabad, about 140 miles from Karachi, are the "wind catchers" on the roofs of most of the houses; the "catcher," a

With its sparkling green fields and snow-capped mountains, the picturesque Swat River Valley, near Peshawar, has often been called "the Switzerland of Asia." Swat, a princely state within Pakistan, is ruled by a Sultan ("Wali"), Miangul Abdul Haq Jahan Zeb. Two of the Sultan's sons are married to daughters of former President Ayub.

crude but effective air-conditioning system, carries the cooling southwest sea breeze down into the rooms of the house.

Semi-arid West Pakistan suffers from a lack of rainfall, which is usually less than 5 inches a year and most of that in the northern hills.

The water buffalo, here seen doing a turn at irrigation, is a familiar sight in Pakistan. Besides serving as draught animal, it provides hides and milk.

13

Bahrain is an attractive resort in the hill country of Pakistan.

Although Bangladesh is quite dry most of the year, the torrential monsoons (southwest winds from the sea) in July through September bring some 100 inches of rainfall that inundate thousands of square miles. During the monsoon season most "pedestrian" traffic moves by boat.

Teal ducks and other wildfowl, such as geese and snipe, lure the hunter to the "hoars" (marshy land) of Sylhet, Bangladesh.

A tribal woman in the Chittagong Hill Tracts attends to her domestic chore of making a thatched roof for her new house. The house itself is built on a bamboo platform over a river.

The Bay of Bengal is a breeding ground for tropical cyclones and tidal waves, which over the centuries have done enormous damage to the Ganges Delta. One of the worst on record took place in November, 1970.

FLORA AND FAUNA

Thanks to heavy rainfall and the presence of water everywhere, Bangladesh boasts many luxuriant, often impenetrable forests. The largest and richest is the Pathatia Reserve Forest. As far as the average Bengali is concerned, the most important tree in his country is the betel nut palm, the fruit of which is chewed with leaf of betel pepper smeared with lime as a narcotic stimulant. The betel stains the mouth a wet scarlet. Since the betel nut palm and the betel pepper vines do not grow in Pakistan, their importation is a prosperous business. Fruit and nut trees include mango, banana, orange, papaya, jack-fruit, and lichee.

The Sundarbans—"the beautiful forest"— where for miles and miles the lofty tree-tops form a virtually unbroken canopy which the sun rarely penetrates, is the home of Bangladesh's most exotic animal life. Here the Royal Bengal tiger swims against the swollen river currents and the crocodile basks on the sun-baked bank. Snakes slither from trees in the noon-day heat and towards evening herds of deer make for the darkening glades while boisterous monkeys shower leaves down upon them from the trees. The forests around Srimangal in the Sylhet district abound with elephants, tigers, leopards, deer, wild hogs, and migratory birds. These animals, as well as rhinoceros and wild buffalo, can also be found in the lush, unexplored jungles of the Chittagong Hill Tracts.

In dry, dusty Pakistan, lovingly-tended

Carrying a deer, two Bengalis return from a shikar (hunt) in the Sundarbans, a forest region entirely surrounded by the mouths of the Ganges and accessible only by water craft. This region, the haunt of the Royal Bengal tiger, attracts many international sportsmen.

flower gardens of hollyhocks, marigolds, snapdragons, roses, dahlias, and phlox provide relief for the citizens' eyes. By contrast to the vast sandy waste that is much of the land of Pakistan, the beautiful Vale of Swat in the northeast is a veritable Garden of Eden. This semi-autonomous state that acceded to Pakistan, with its lush green fields and fruit orchards rising in mountainside terraces, is reminiscent of Switzerland.

The traditional beasts of burden are oxen and water buffalo in Bangladesh, and oxen, camels, horses, and donkeys in Pakistan.

Vultures, a common sight in Pakistan, are ever ready to descend on the carcass of an ox, a goat or a water buffalo.

The watery reaches of the Sundarbans in the Ganges delta abound with big fish.

NATURAL RESOURCES

Pakistan is handicapped by a relative scarcity of natural resources needed for economic development. Although the production of oil has increased sixfold since independence, the total output is still extremely small—as compared to adjacent Iran's enormous annual production. As the search for oil continues,

however, the experts are not without hope. A major exploration project now in progress is being carried out by a government-owned corporation with assistance from Russia. The work is financed by a substantial Soviet loan made in 1961 and employs Soviet technicians and equipment. Several private oil companies have also been engaged in explorations, and some are still exploring on a limited basis.

While searching for oil, large reserves of natural gas were discovered in both East and West Pakistan. Gas is being produced and utilized in both sections of the country for power, fertilizer, and petro-chemicals. Although there are coal deposits as well, the coal is of a poor grade, containing a large proportion of sulphur. Total production is less than 30 per cent of Pakistan's requirements.

Mineral deposits include: limestone, gypsum, rock salt, chromite, barite, asbestos, antimony, magnesite, and silica. Of the metallic minerals, only chromite and barite are in sufficient supply to be commercially mined, and of these only chromite is exported.

The wildlife of Pakistan is always in great demand by zoos all over the world. Here a young cheetah puts up a last-minute fight before being crated for his jet flight to London.

The Shalimar Gardens in Lahore were built in 1641 by Shah Jahan the Glorious and was the site of many a sumptuous Royal Family outing. Today, the beautifully-tended gardens, an unsurpassed example of Mogul landscape design, attract millions of Pakistanis and tourists.

2. THE HISTORY

THE IMMEDIATE ORIGINS OF the concept of Pakistan as an independent nation for the Moslems of the Indian subcontinent are to be found in certain events that took place in British India in the last half century. Indirectly, however, the seeds of the new nation were planted hundreds of years ago.

The early history of what is now Pakistan is the history of India, and the original ethnic and cultural elements of both countries are the same: an ancient pre-Aryan civilization con- quered about 1500 B.C. by Aryan invaders from the northwest. The Aryans, related in language to most of the peoples of Europe, mingled with their more advanced predecessors such as the Dravidians and developed the Hindu religion and the Indic languages. One of the pre-Aryan tongues, Brahui, still survives in a corner of Pakistan; dominant languages of the country— Urdu, Sindhi, Baluchi, Pushtu, and Punjabi are all Indic as is Bengali, the language of Bangladesh. Today, the Aryan strain is strongly

At the Jaince Mosque in Rawalpindi, several Pakistanis bathe their feet in a reflecting pool while, in the background, others kneel, facing Mecca, to pray. One of the main duties of every Moslem, as clearly stated in the Koran, is the necessity of praying five times a day. It is not necessary to go to a mosque to pray; a prayer rug may be put down anywhere, indoors or out, but the faithful must always face Mecca. On Friday, the day on which Moslems usually go to the mosque, all business houses and offices are closed in the afternoon.

This bas-relief is a replica of a seal found at Mohenjo-daro. Built of soft brick, the old city is now in danger of crumbling, due to Indus Valley irrigation projects, which have raised the subsoil water level.

evident in Pakistan, many of whose light-skinned people closely resemble Europeans. The earliest beginnings of Pakistan are to be found in the introduction of Islam into India.

This small sculpture, possibly the head of a king or priest, was unearthed at Mohenjo-daro and is on display at a museum adjacent to the ancient ruins.

Moslem sailors first landed on the shores of Sind early in the 7th century during the lifetime of the Prophet Mohammed, a camel-driver of Mecca whose divine revelation in visions were embodied in the Koran, the holy book of the new religion he founded and called Islam.

Then, as now, the majority of people living in India were Hindus and, from the very first, it was obvious that Islam and Hinduism stood in marked contrast to each other. Previous invaders of the subcontinent had been on a more primitive level than the Indians and had therefore been easily absorbed into the Hindu system. But the Moslems, with their confident new religion, could not be brushed aside as barbarians and, although from the beginning there was mutual influence upon both religions, there could be no fusion.

The Moslem population increased with the migration of many Turks and Afghans, who settled in India and either sent for their families or intermarried locally. Many Hindus were also converted to the new religion by the Sufis, dedicated men who devoted their lives to the study and spread of Islam, speaking to the hearts of all through the symbolic Persian poetry of Ferid-ed-Din Attar, Hafiz, and Omar Khayyam.

A number of group conversions took place

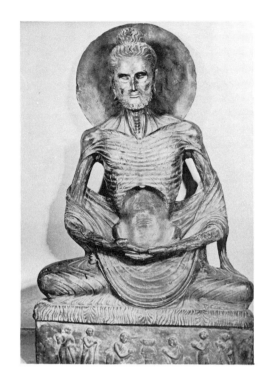

all over north India, while a mass conversion occurred in East Bengal (now Bangladesh), where the Moslems brought relief to many outcaste communities from the domination and social restriction maintained by the Brahmins, the highest of the Hindu castes. Hindu society from early times had been divided into rigid layers. A man was born into a certain caste, married within it, and all his life was governed by a set of rules peculiar to it. The caste-free code of Islam had an immediate appeal to many lower-caste Hindus.

The main impact of Islam upon India, however, must be credited to the semi-barbaric Turkish tribes that invaded India at the end of the 11th century, conquering the Punjab, which, with a few interludes, has been Moslem-dominated ever since. In the 12th century, Delhi fell to Muhammad of Ghor, and the Turkish empire in India began. Over the next two centuries, the Turks, who carried their Moslem religion wherever they carried their victorious arms, overthrew Brahmin rule in

Bengal and the powers of the Rajputs, the warrior caste that held sway in north and central India. They struck the death blow to organized Buddhism, already in deep decline, by the massacre of the Buddhist monks and the razing of their temples. Buddhism, an outgrowth of Hinduism, had for a time been the dominant religion of the subcontinent, but had lost influence after 200 B.C. Although the Turks could not break up Hinduism itself, they did manage to hinder it by depriving it of state patronage.

THE MOGUL EMPERORS

Toward the end of the 14th century, the Turkish empire disintegrated under a flood of dynastic disputes. In 1398, it collapsed altogether when the great Mongol conqueror, Timur (known in literature as Tamerlane) and

21

Ruined mosques and tombs from the Mogul period can be found at Tatta, 65 miles from Karachi. Here there are an estimated 1,000,000 graves contained in six square miles of earth.

his Golden Horde took and sacked Delhi. The century following this disastrous raid was, for India, one of economic and political collapse, a dark period of local dynasties, power struggles, revolution, and violent death.

In 1505, Babur, a descendent of Genghis Khan and Timur and the first of the Mogul Emperors, invaded the subcontinent. By 1529, all of northern India had submitted to him. The Moslem conqueror, who was to die only one year later, laid the foundations for the Mogul Empire, the most splendid ever to rule over India. It reached the height of its power and wealth under the wise and able rule of Babur's grandson, Akbar, who held the reins of power from 1556 to 1605. Akbar cultivated the good will of the Hindus, especially the Rajputs, who had never ceased to rebel against Moslem rule. Akbar included many Hindus in high governmental positions and he made no attempt to convert them to Islam. In order to create peace and harmony between the Moslems and the Hindus, he encouraged intermarriages among the Rajputs and the Moguls.

Akbar's son, Jahangir, became Emperor in 1605. Like his father, he respected the religions of others. It was Jahangir who granted permission to the English East India Company for the building of a factory in India.

The reign of Jahangir's son, Shah Jahan the Glorious, lasted from 1628 to 1658, perhaps the greatest period of the Mogul Empire. Following the tolerant religious policies of his forebears, Shah Jahan is best remembered for

Old tombs rise starkly from the arid plain at Choukhandi, near Karachi.

22

The balanced design of Mogul architecture is well illustrated by the gateway of the Badshahi Mosque in Lahore.

his influence on Mogul architecture, the best-known examples of which are the Taj Mahal in Agra, India, and the beautiful Shalimar Gardens in Lahore, Pakistan.

The last of the Mogul emperors was Aurangzeb, who ruled from 1658 to 1707. The third son of Shah Jahan the Glorious, Aurangzeb, regarding himself as the leader of a Moslem state rather than the monarch of all India, was an intolerant ruler who persecuted the Hindus by razing their temples and taxing them heavily. When he died in 1707, the Mogul dynasty died with him, leaving an almost permanent rupture in Moslem-Hindu relations. Once again, India broke up into many separate kingdoms, some Hindu and some Moslem. All was chaos as these rivals proceeded to tear each other to pieces, falling out even among themselves. These regional rivalries played into the hands of the French and British who, for many years, had been jockeying for control over India and its lucrative trade. The British, under General Robert Clive, scored a decisive victory

Elaborate mosaics of convex glass pieces gleam as radiantly today as they did centuries ago in the Shish Mahal (The Hall of Mirrors) in the famous Lahore Fort. The Fort owes its strength and beauty to Mogul Emperor Akbar, who made Lahore his headquarters in 1585 and rebuilt the Fort from its frame of mud into solid masonry. Akbar's sons and grandsons all made exquisite additions to it during their lifetimes.

19th century, the British East India Company ruled nearly the entire subcontinent.

"FIRST WAR OF INDEPENDENCE"

Pakistanis call The Sepoy Mutiny of 1857–8 their first war of independence. The mutiny occurred among the sepoys, Bengali soldiers who served under British officers in the East India Company's army. Somehow the story spread among them that the cartridges of their new Enfield rifles were greased with animal fat. The Hindu sepoys believed it to be beef fat and were enraged because Hindus by religion hold cows sacred; the Moslems were convinced that it was pork fat and were enraged because religious law forbids Moslems to eat or touch pigs. Reports and suspicions that the British meant to deliberately break their religious taboos touched off a series of frenzied outbursts of violence. After successfully quelling the rebellion, the British government took full

over the French at Arcot (near Madras) in 1751, and another over the Nawab (ruler) of Bengal at Plassey in 1757.

Just as Indian disunity had made the subcontinent prey to Moslem conquest, so too had it paved the way for British conquest. From 1757 on, Britain steadily widened the areas under its control until, by the middle of the

These ancient watchtowers once protected the outskirts of Lahore. Today they have been replaced by modern radar.

control of India from the East India Company. In 1877, the British Prime Minister, Benjamin Disraeli, succeeded in having Queen Victoria formally crowned as Empress of India.

Opposition to British rule formed slowly at first. Moslem and Hindu leaders began to agitate for an effective voice in Indian affairs and, in 1885, the Indian National Congress was formed. The original aim of the Congress was merely self-rule within the British Empire, but not total independence. Its membership was chiefly Hindu. Although Moslems formed the second largest element in India's population, they were greatly outnumbered by the Hindus and felt a need for guarantees to protect their minority rights. On the issue of these rights, Moslem leaders were unable to reach agreement with their Hindu colleagues in the National Congress. To present their position more effectively, a number of Moslem leaders formed the All India Muslim League in 1906.

MOHAMMED ALI JINNAH

More than any other person, Mohammed Ali Jinnah, a British-educated lawyer who headed the Muslim League from 1916, is revered by Pakistanis as Quaid-i-Azam, or father of his country.

Under Jinnah's leadership, the League, a small, weak body that was splintered by the internal dissension and angry outbursts of its members, gained strength and prestige. Jinnah strongly advocated Hindu-Moslem unity and, like Mahatma Gandhi who headed the Indian National Congress, he advocated a united, independent state. Perhaps no one was more shocked than Jinnah when the famed poet and philosopher, Muhammad Iqbal, in the course of an address to the League in 1930, put forward the suggestion that the Moslems in northwest India should form a separate Moslem state. But as Jinnah grew more and more disillusioned with Gandhi's extremist policies and more and more convinced that his fellow Moslems would never attain their rights in a united India that was predominantly Hindu, he decided to devote all his energies to translating the poet's dream of a separate Moslem state into a reality.

The Moslems declaration of independence, the Lahore Resolution, was passed on March

Mohammed Ali Jinnah was the first Governor-General of independent Pakistan.

23, 1940, a date that is now a national holiday called Pakistan Day. The Resolution declared that, in any future governmental arrangement between Britain and India, "the areas in which the Moslems are numerically a majority, as in the northwestern and eastern zones of India, should be grouped to constitute Independent States." Jinnah, at that time, vowed that no power on earth could prevent Pakistan. Gandhi dismissed the entire idea as absurd and suggested that Jinnah was suffering from hallucinations.

During World War II, the Hindu's National Congress refused to co-operate with Great Britain, Gandhi and other party leaders choosing to withdraw from the Indian government rather than be drawn automatically into a war that was opposed to their policy of non-violence. The Muslim League, on the other hand, supported the British fully, hoping to gain greater consideration after the war for the rights of the Moslem community.

25

INDEPENDENCE AND PARTITION

Britain's economic and military weakness after World War II, plus the cumulative effect of India's long-standing demand for self-government convinced the British Labour Party that the time had come for Indian independence. The National Congress and the Muslim League were unable to agree, however, either on the terms for drafting a constitution or on the method for establishing an interim government. The split between the two groups was so great that no settlement short of partition could be reached.

In 1946, as talk of partition swept throughout India, communal riots broke out. People were confused about which country they would belong to, what would happen to them if they were in a majority or a minority in their community. Finally, on June 3, 1947, Britain announced a plan to establish two nations— India, with a Hindu majority, and Pakistan, with a Moslem majority. Under British rule India had been divided into British Provinces, ruled directly by the Crown, and princely states, whose rulers owed allegiance to the Crown, and which were, in effect, protectorates. Pakistan was to consist of the Moslem-majority areas of British India; Bengal and the

Punjab were to be partitioned, and many princely states were to be free to join either nation or to remain independent. Pakistan thus became a sovereign independent nation within the British Commonwealth on August 14, 1947.

Partition, particularly of the Punjab, was accompanied by bloody communal rioting as over 10,000,000 people tried to move across the new boundaries to the country of their choice. It was one of the greatest exoduses in human history; the number of refugees who were killed in transit will never be known, but it has been estimated that 500,000 Moslems alone died as their new nation was being born.

Under incredible circumstances, the government of the Dominion of Pakistan opened for business in its first capital, Karachi. Hastily erected tents served as government buildings, rough tables and boxes substituted as furniture, and the sleepy seaport had to be scoured for paper and pencils. Mohammed Ali Jinnah became the first Governor-General of Pakistan. Liaquat Ali Khan served as his Prime Minister.

THE KASHMIR DISPUTE

Two independent states ruled by Moslem princes but with Hindu majorities acceded to India. The princely state of Jammu and Kashmir, with a predominately Moslem population ruled by a Hindu prince, refused at first to join either India or Pakistan. Some of the Moslem subjects, supported by fanatical Moslem tribesmen from Pakistan, revolted against their Hindu leader, who thereupon offered to accede to India in return for military assistance to repel the Pakistani invaders. India accepted the accession on the condition that Kashmir's ultimate status would depend on the expressed will of the people.

India took its dispute with Pakistan over Kashmir to the United Nations on January 1, 1948, and a year later the United Nations succeeded in arranging a cease-fire along a line roughly dividing the area in half but leaving two-thirds of the population under Indian control. Pakistan still claims that the Hindu prince has ignored the desires of the predominantly Moslem population and continues to press for a plebiscite—a vote by all the people of Kashmir to see which nation they want to belong to. The United Nations has also supported the idea of a plebiscite but India refuses outright and continues to treat Kashmir as an Indian state.

DEATH OF JINNAH

In September, 1948, Mohammed Ali Jinnah died, a little more than one year after the establishment of the nation for which he had fought so long and hard. His birthday, December 25, is a national holiday in Pakistan.

Jinnah was succeeded as Governor-General by Khwaja Nazimuddin of East Pakistan. The political instability that followed brought frequent party realignments and cabinet changes in the central government as well as in the provinces. No one could reach any agreement about what it meant to be a Moslem nation and the people, no longer unified, again thought of themselves as Bengalis, Punjabis, and Sindhis instead of Pakistanis. A severe blow was dealt to the nation's fortunes in October, 1951, when Prime Minister Liaquat Ali Khan, a popular, competent, long-time associate of Jinnah, was assassinated. Within the next seven years, Pakistan had six prime ministers. With no leaders of Jinnah's or Liaquat's stature to unite the country, Pakistan could not effect the kind of stability that was so necessary for progress.

In 1956, after years of bickering and disagreement, a new constitution was finally adopted. Pakistan made the change from a nominal monarchy and became the Islamic Republic of Pakistan, electing to stay with the Commonwealth. The first President of the Republic was Iskander Mirza. Under corrupt elected representatives who used their positions for their own good, the economy virtually collapsed, the people lost confidence in one another and in their nation, and the pulse of Pakistan was at its lowest ebb.

A BLOODLESS REVOLUTION

In 1958, a group of senior military officers who, up to then, had avoided direct political involvement, considered it necessary to take control of the nation's affairs. On October 7, President Mirza, supported by the Army Commander-in-Chief, General Ayub Khan and other senior officers, proclaimed a "peaceful revolution." The President declared martial law, dismissed both central and provincial governments, and suspended the Constitution;

At one of the forts at the Khyber Pass near the Afghan frontier, members of the Khyber Rifles Regiment line up for morning inspection.

27

he then left for England. Without shedding a single drop of blood, General Ayub Khan had become a military dictator. The day on which he took office, October 27, is now a national holiday called Revolution Day.

Ayub's aim, as he told the people in his first address to the nation, was to restore democracy, "but of a type that people can understand and make work." Ayub's administration effected many, much-needed reforms. Corrupt politicians were either jailed or replaced by competent people. A land-reform scheme was instituted, limiting a landowner to 500 acres of irrigated land or 1,000 acres of unirrigated land; this was especially important to the farmers of West Pakistan where, before land reform, 15 per cent of the total cultivable area was held by less than 1 per cent of the landowners. Changes in the laws granted equal rights to women, including the right to run for government office; family laws were changed so that a husband could no longer divorce his wife merely by declaring, "I divorce you." Many new schools and universities were opened to combat the problem of illiteracy. Other important new projects were designed to improve health, industry, commerce, electrical power, defence, and communications.

In 1962, a new constitution was adopted and, as Ayub had promised at the time of the military take-over, the dictatorship ended. Martial law was suspended, political parties were once again allowed to function, and a new presidential election was scheduled for 1965. In that election, Ayub defeated his opponent, 70-year-old Fatima Jinnah, the well-loved, well-respected sister of Mohammed Ali Jinnah.

In 1969, President Ayub resigned due to failing health, and was succeeded by General A. M. Yahya Khan.

President Yahya Khan indicated that steps would be taken to give East Pakistan a greater share in the government. He called for elections for a constituent assembly to draft a new constitution. The elections were held in December, 1970.

Before they took place, East Pakistan was ravaged by the terrible cyclone of November, 1970—one of the worst disasters of modern times. Aid from West Pakistan was too little and

Dwarfing all other political leaders, President Mohammed Ayub Khan sustained himself by the sheer force of his extraordinary personality.

too late. Dissatisfaction with the central government was so great that when the elections took place, the Awami Party of East Pakistan gained a clear majority in the National Assembly. This meant that Sheikh Mujibur Rahman, leader of the Awami Party, would be the next prime minister of the divided nation, after the constitutional assembly convened in March, 1971. "Mujib," as the Awami leader is popularly known, had long advocated a self-governing "Bangla Desh" (Bengal State).

This prospect was too much for the West Pakistanis. President Yahya postponed the constitutional assembly and started a troop build-up in East Pakistan. In March, 1971, civil war broke out in East Pakistan. The government suppressed the rebellion ruthlessly from the outset. By late 1971, it was estimated that nearly 8,000,000 East Pakistani refugees had crossed the border into India. Famine and epidemic disease threatened those who remained. The two regions of Pakistan were never farther apart.

Following the secession of Bangladesh, in December, 1971, Yahya Khan resigned, and was succeeded by Zulfikar Ali Bhutto.

Modern and traditional architectural motifs are harmoniously blended in the Pakistan House of the new capital at Islamabad. This spacious planned city, in the foothills of the Himalayas near Rawalpindi, drew on the talents of architects all over the world.

3. THE GOVERNMENT

IN FEBRUARY, 1967, when President Mohammad Ayub Khan's nagging cold hardened into influenza and then viral pneumonia, the Government of Pakistan virtually ground to a complete halt. Ayub's serious illness and the resultant suspended animation in the government served as a potent reminder to the world of how much Pakistan was essentially a one-man show.

While readily admitting that the President gave Pakistan political stability for over a decade, his opponents—and many of his supporters—criticize him for failing to establish an institution of government that has any likelihood of handling a presidential succession in orderly fashion.

Muzzling all opposition, the President kept so firm a grip on the country and the Government that no other political figure was allowed to attain national stature. In the political vacuum that he created, the question that loomed large was "After Ayub Khan, who?" That question has been answered, but many problems inherited from Ayub Khan faced his successor, General Yahya Khan.

"BASIC DEMOCRACIES"

The present Government of Pakistan is federal and presidential in form. The President, who has wide executive powers under the constitution, selects his Cabinet and is Supreme Commander of the military forces. (The key to Ayub Khan's autocratic power was his powerful army.) The National Assembly had 156 mem-

29

The Pakistan National Assembly is seen in session in Karachi, before the seat of government was moved first to Rawalpindi, then to Islamabad.

bers, divided equally between East and West Pakistan. The central government had exclusive power to make laws on defence and foreign affairs, trade and commerce, banking, insurance, and telecommunications.

The two provincial governments were headed by a Governor chosen by the President. The Governor was aided by a provincial cabinet of his own choosing. Each provincial assembly had 155 members, with five seats usually reserved for women. The provincial governments had jurisdiction over all residual matters.

In 1960, Ayub instituted his system of Basic Democracies to establish a uniform local government structure throughout the country and to provide local experience in self-government. Under this system, the population was divided into units of about 1,000 in West Pakistan and 1,250 in East Pakistan, figures that roughly corresponded to the size of

a typical Pakistani village. The people of each village-size unit vote for a local person, whom they know and trust, to represent them in a union council that administers affairs for about 10 such units. Each union council in turn elects a chairman, who represents his region on the next higher council, and so on through district and divisional levels. By four such steps, or tiers—Village Union, Tehsil/Thana Council, District Council, and Divisional Council—the President and representatives to the National Assembly are elected.

Since June, 1962, when Ayub lifted the ban on political activity and political parties, several parties have been formed and other political groups are active. The Muslim League—the founding party of Pakistan—is now divided into two principal parties. The supporters of Ayub formed the Pakistan Muslim League, which obtained majorities in the central and two provincial assemblies. The other main

The Government of Pakistan assumes full responsibility for the health of the nation. At present, there are about 17,000 practicing doctors and surgeons, with 12 medical colleges training about 1,000 doctors a year, and 26 training schools turning out some 350 nurses annually.

branch of the old Muslim League is the Council Muslim League. In 1967, six opposition parties joined to form the Pakistan Democratic Movement, united only in its opposition to Ayub and his "Basic Democracy" system. The sole plank of its platform called for the direct election of the President and the National Assembly with all citizens voting, and abolition of the electoral college of 120,000 Basic Democrats.

INTERNAL STRIFE

The greatest problem that faced President Ayub Khan—and the one that has hopelessly complicates Pakistan's difficulties—was the resentment that had been building up in East Pakistan, where the people were not yet convinced that they were regarded as equals of West Pakistanis. The Bengalis of East Pakistan felt that they were continually being short-changed by a power structure in West Pakistan.

Ayub's opponents asserted that the Eastern province received less than a full share of development funds, jobs in the Civil Service, and appointments in the army.

Independence movements sprang up periodically in East Bengal but they were put down by Ayub's government without difficulty. Ayub encountered nothing resembling the disastrous uprising that his successor, Yahya, was to face.

Ayub also faced bitter, undisguised opposition in most of the major cities, particularly in Karachi, where he lost the affection of the people when he moved the capital from that city to Rawalpindi and, later, to Islamabad. In the 1965 election, Ayub failed to carry the Karachi vote. His opponents charged that corruption permeated every level of the government. Inflation and the spiralling cost of living, as well as a general let-down over the stalemate with India on the disputed territory of

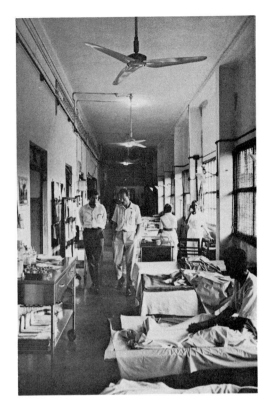

Kashmir constituted other problems for Ayub. The principal shortcoming of the opposition to Ayub was the absence of a single person under whom the groups were able to unite.

Yahya Khan's unyielding stand towards the legitimate wishes of the Bengalis led to the break-up of Pakistan. His successor, Zulfikar Ali Bhutto, assumed control of a weakened nation. The several nationalities making up what was left of Pakistan began to sprout secessionist movements—notably in Sind, Baluchistan and the Pathan districts.

FOREIGN AFFAIRS

Pakistan is the only nation in South Asia which, by virtue of its membership in the Southeast Asia Treaty Organization and the Central Treaty Organization, has openly aligned itself with the West. The relations between Pakistan and the United States developed a distinct chill, however, in the fall of 1965 when open hostilities began with India along the line of demarcation in Kashmir, and the United

To provide more fertilizer for the nation's farmers, Pakistan and the United States financed the construction of factories which now produce more than 300,000 tons of chemical fertilizer each year.

States suspended military and economic aid to both countries. In the Pakistanis' view, their American allies deserted them in the fighting with India over Kashmir. Although relations between the two countries took a somewhat warmer turn after the United States resumed military and economic assistance, Pakistan, in recent years, has become increasingly critical of the United States and has sought to broaden its ties with the Afro-Asian countries and Communist China.

Relations between India and Pakistan reflect centuries-old Hindu-Moslem rivalry. In addition to the continued dispute over Kashmir, other important issues between India and Pakistan include the division of water from the rivers flowing into Pakistan from Indian-controlled territory; inadequately defined or or marked borders between the two countries; several economic and financial problems stemming from the 1947 partition; and the problem of the settlement of refugees who continue to move from one country to the other. Some

progress has been made in settling these disputes, but relations are still periodically strained.

Relations with Afghanistan have long been complicated by the controversy over the Pushtu-speaking Pathans who live both in Pakistan and across the northern border in Afghanistan. The Afghan government firmly insists that a separate, independent state should be established for all Pathans now included in Pakistan. In 1961, the two countries broke off diplomatic relations over this issue, with Pakistan taking the position that Afghan claims to an interest in the status of people in Pakistan constituted interference in its internal affairs. With the assistance of the Shah of Iran, the countries re-established relations in 1963.

When East Pakistan became independent as Bangladesh, it immediately applied for membership in the Commonwealth. When, early in 1972, it became certain that Bangladesh would be admitted, Pakistan withdrew from the Commonwealth.

Pakistani farm workers rest on charpoys in the shade of a courtyard.

4. THE PEOPLE

THE POPULATION of Pakistan was estimated to be 51,000,000 in 1973. The exact figure for Bangladesh is not certain, but a 1972 estimate placed it as high as 75,000,000.

In any case, Bangladesh has one of the world's most crowded populations and, if the birth rate of 3 per cent annually is not checked, the present population will have doubled by 1985. The situation is most critical in Bangladesh, which has a population density rate of

A family rests by the roadside in front of a sign in Urdu urging the application of family planning. It stands as a silent reminder that drastic steps must be taken to balance the exploding population with the potential food supply.

The hard, lean body of a Bengali dock worker reflects a lifetime of hard work.

The Aryan element in Pakistan is well illustrated by this blue-eyed man from the Pathan region.

1,100 people per square mile. The Government has undertaken strong measures to bring all sections of the population to realize the absolute importance of family planning.

Pakistan, with its pageant of people descended from Afghan, Turkish, Tartar, and Aryan invaders as well as the Macedonian deserters from the army of Alexander the Great, is a

A free mobile medical dispensary makes regular visits to small village market places to help combat leprosy.

state of many languages and ethnic groups. Though diverse in customs and temperament, the people are united in their faith in Islam.

The majority of Pakistanis and Bengalis are small, brown-skinned, and fine-featured; the Bengalis, who have a greater degree of non-Aryan blood, are physically distinguishable from their former countrymen, tending to be smaller and darker. The wild, unexplored region of the Chittagong Hill Tracts, Bangladesh, is the habitat of primitive tribes of Mongolian extraction, called the "Children of the River"; the largest tribe, numbering 125,000, is that of the Buddhist Chakmas, advanced people who scorn the backward tribes of the Moghs, Murungs, and Kukis. The most fascinating tribesmen of Pakistan are, no doubt, the fierce war-like Pathans who live near the Afghan border.

The Pathan tribesmen of Pakistan, tall, war-like, and extremely religious, have always been fiercely jealous of their liberty. Their curious code imposes three obligations upon them—giving asylum to any refugee who demands it even if that refugee be a mortal enemy; extending hospitality to all strangers; and securing revenge for any slight.

Although the vast majority of people live in small villages scattered throughout the country, Pakistan does have many major cities. Karachi, with its population of over 2,700,000, is the largest city and principal port. In 1947, one American writer described Karachi as "a one-camel town." The small fishing port sweltering on the Arabian Sea has come a long way since then. Boasting one of the finest airports and many modern new buildings, it is now an important financial hub. About 750 miles from Karachi is Lahore, with a population of slightly over 1,600,000, the second largest city. It is the nation's cultural and academic headquarters, and the site of over 40 colleges and institutions, including the famed Punjab University. Rawalpindi (population 432,000), more affectionately known as "Pindi," was the former military headquarters of the British in the Punjab and it still retains a Kiplingesque atmosphere. Other important cities of Pakistan include Hyderabad (population 620,000), important commercially, and Peshawar (popu-

On a street in Dacca, two Moslem women appear in the "burqa," an ankle-length garment with slits for the eyes that is worn in public by women observing "purdah." Purdah is the Islamic custom of keeping women secluded from all men except their very close relatives.

This Pakistani woman visiting the Shalimar Gardens wears a graceful silk sari—a piece of cloth six yards long that is folded and draped into a dress. Although the majority of women in Bangladesh wear the sari, in Pakistan it is worn more in the large cities than in the villages.

Men from the Pathan region perform the vigorous "khattak," a sword dance performed to the music of pipes and drums.

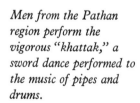

Dacca has over 700 mosques, but the Star Mosque, located in the oldest quarter of the city, is considered by many to be the gem of them all.

lation 200,000), located on an ancient caravan trail near the border of Afghanistan. The three largest cities of Bangladesh are Dacca (population 740,000), the capital of the country and known as the "city of mosques and muslins"; Chittagong (population 300,000), a picturesque seaport on green hills overlooking the Bay of Bengal; and Cox's Bazaar, a seaside resort popular for bathing, fishing, hunting and shopping.

RELIGION

Pakistan was created so that the Moslems of the subcontinent could have a homeland of their own. Today, according to the latest estimate, 97 per cent of the population is Moslem. Under the country's constitution, the President must be a Moslem, and all laws must be in accordance with the precepts and principles of Islam.

The spread of the Moslem religion after its founding by Mohammed was phenomenally rapid in the 7th and 8th centuries and it was soon dominant from Spain to India. The message from God to Mohammed was transmitted by the angel Gabriel and is known as the Koran, the sacred book of Islam which contains an immense body of laws and regulations to be followed by the faithful. Even though many Pakistanis cannot read the Koran, they can recite it from memory. Since the Koran

At the Quissa Khawani Bazaar in Peshawar, a group of men pass the time with gossip and tall tales. In the old days the Bazaar site was a camping ground for caravans where professional story-tellers recited ballads and tales of war.

The Chandanpura Mosque at Chittagong is a fanciful interpretation of traditional Moslem architecture.

the Hindu temples are beautifully and elaborately decorated with figures of their gods—Brahma, Vishnu, Krishna, Shiva, and Kali. Other minority religions include Christians (700,000), Buddhists in Bangladesh (400,000), and Parsees (5,000), most of whom live in Karachi.

LANGUAGE AND LITERATURE

Tourists from the West are often amazed and delighted to discover that many Pakistanis speak and write English. This is yet another reminder that the British once ruled the subcontinent, at which time English was the language of the government. It is still taught in most schools and colleges and, until 1970, it remained an official language of Pakistan.

Shortly after partition, the government of Pakistan sought to establish its own national language. This proved to be no easy task for, while Bengali is the mother tongue of Bangladesh, the people of Pakistan speak

forbids the making of any images of God (Allah), the many magnificent mosques of Pakistan are decorated only with abstract designs.

Pakistanis, no doubt remembering their own experience as a minority religion prior to partition, pride themselves on their tolerant attitude towards the people of other religions. Their green-and-white national flag, in fact, symbolizes this religious unity, the green representing the Moslems, the white representing the people of other beliefs.

MINORITIES

The largest group of non-Moslems is made up of over 10,000,000 Bengali Hindus. Although they are relatively few in Pakistan, one out of every seven Bengalis is a Hindu.

Like the Moslems' Koran, the Hindus' holy books—the Rig Veda, the Bhagavad Gita, and the Ramayana—set down the rules of conduct for daily living. Unlike the Moslem's mosque,

A monk, in his distinctive yellow robe, poses before the Buddhist temple at Ramu in the Cox's Bazaar subdivision of Bangladesh. Buddhists dye their robes in a mixture of water and saffron.

A man staggers under the weight of a colossal burden on the streets of Lahore. Manpower is one of the cheapest, most available commodities in this part of the world.

This little girl wears a ring in her nose as an ornament, a not uncommon embellishment on the Indian subcontinent.

many different mother tongues and dialects. The three main language groups are Punjabi, Pushtu, and Sindhi; the dialects within these groups are so varied that the inhabitants of Multan cannot be easily understood by the people of Lahore, even though both speak a form of Punjabi and live less than 200 miles apart. The government decided that there should be two national languages—Bengali for East Pakistan and Urdu for West Pakistan. Urdu was selected because it can be readily understood by people of many different mother tongues. A relatively new speech, Urdu is actually a blend of many languages and dialects with Hindi as its primary base. It was developed by the Persian, Turkish, and Arabic invading armies. This very crude barracks "lingo" was

This young boy sports the familiar Pakistani cap of karakul (Persian lamb) that is worn by most men. It is usually called the Jinnah cap, in memory of Mohammed Ali Jinnah who helped popularize the style.

Pakistanis and foreign visitors throng the National Horse and Cattle Show, one of the attractions of historic Lahore, the former provincial capital of West Pakistan.

gradually refined and its use became widespread. Urdu is written from right to left in Arabic script. Bengali is written from left to right in Sanskritic characters.

Of all literary forms, Pakistanis are most fond of poetry. It is quite natural to them to commit to memory long passages from the works of their most popular poets—Shah Abdul Latif, Khushal Khan Khattak, Muhammad Iqbal, Waris Shah, names that are quite unfamiliar to Westerners. A popular form of entertainment, especially among educated people, is the *mushaira*, which is similar to a poetry reading in New York's Greenwich Village or London's

A dancing girl of the Manipuri tribe, one of the hill groups of Bangladesh and adjacent parts of India, poses in her traditional costume. Manipuris perform many dances that unfold love themes rooted in ancient mythology, during the Festival of the Full Moon (Rash Leela) in February and the Festival of Colours (Doljatra) in April.

Idal-Fitr, signifying the end of Ramazan, the Moslem's month of fasting, is a day of happiness in Pakistan—a day of special sweets, new clothes, the sharing of food, and the greeting of old friends. These carefree young ladies in their gaily printed new gowns swing in the spirit of the day.

A bride (left) wears the traditional costume. Marriages are arranged by Pakistani parents who agree on the dowry with the "naushah" (new king), as the bridegroom is called. There is usually no official at the ceremony since, legally, the couple simply need to consent to be married before witnesses.

Chelsea. A group of 20 or more people gathers to read their own poetry to one another, in sessions that can go on for four to six hours.

ARTS AND CRAFTS

Pakistanis and Bengalis excel in the arts of painting, weaving, poetry, music, and dance. Working on crude hand looms, villagers weave fine muslins just as their ancestors did through many generations and, when the cloth is done, they paint or stamp bright, fanciful designs on them by hand. Potters shape useful clay utensils by hand while an assistant turns the old-fashioned potter's wheel. Embroidery, leather work, and miniature painting continue to be fine arts. Music, whether it be the intimate and deeply philosophic classical work or the rich, characteristic folk music of the countryside, forms another great delight of the people and with it, the dance, both the graceful village

dances of Bangladesh and the vigorous *luddi* and *khattak* dances of Pakistan.

Many of Pakistan's modern artists, such as

In Karachi, a snake-charmer's thin, reedy piping proves charming enough to a fascinated cobra.

A display of equestrian acrobatics is one of the highlights of Lahore's famed Horse and Cattle Show. Held annually, usually from February 15 through March 10, the exhibition is staged in an enormous stadium patterned after a Mogul fortress.

Abdul Rahman Chugtai, are still influenced by the art introduced to the country by the Great Mogul emperors, whose tombs, gardens, and mosques still beautify the country, an influence that extends even to the nation's architecture.

SPORTS AND PASTIMES

In cricket, wrestling, hockey, polo, and athletics, Pakistan has achieved international distinction. According to Pakistani historians,

Night clubs, as we know them, are not found in Pakistan. All the leading hotels, however, have Western-type bar-rooms and cabarets. At the Kohsaar Supper Club in the Intercontinental Rawalpindi Hotel, an Italian rock-and-roll group provides entertainment while patrons may dine on either Pakistani specialties or international cuisine.

achieved a record swimming the English Channel.

Pakistan also has games more local in character, such as *kabbadi*, a catching game in which nimble young boys, wearing nothing but loincloths, their bodies made slick by oil, try to outwit and out-race one another. Pakistanis are fond of hunting, with gun, camera, or falcon, and Bangladesh is considered to be the hunter's paradise on earth.

Children of both sexes are encouraged at a very early age to take up games in order to develop their bodies and to learn the necessary art of losing cheerfully and winning gracefully.

EDUCATION

With the primary purpose of turning out young men and women capable of doing a practical job and making a practical contribution to the advancement and prosperity of the country, the Government of Pakistan has given education a high priority. An all-out improvement is being sought in the quality of education at all levels—to make it more practical, less bookish, and more appropriate to the necessities of the times and of the nation. In addition to his usual studies, each student is required to do

A marked upsurge in Pakistan's tourist trade took place after the 1962 visit of Jacqueline Kennedy, then First Lady of the United States. Mrs. Kennedy and her sister, Princess Lee Radziwill, were helped aboard a camel owned by Bashir the Camel Driver, who soon afterward became a celebrity in his own right when he accepted an invitation to the United States from Lyndon B. Johnson, then Vice President.

the ancient Persian sport of polo survived in Gilgit and nearby valleys long after its popularity waned elsewhere during the 16th century. The game was rediscovered by British officers posted to India and once again it spread throughout the world. One of the sports highlights of the year is the famed National Horse and Cattle Show at Lahore, an impressive spectacle that includes polo, trick riding, acrobatics, and performing horses. Swimming, particularly in Bangladesh with its many rivers and waterways, is also greatly enjoyed, and it was Pakistan's own Brojen Das who

Students pore over books in the library at the College of Social Welfare and Research in Dacca. Graduates eventually staff numerous social welfare schemes throughout the country.

43

Undergraduates handle complicated equipment as part of their practical work at the Engineering College, Peshawar. To a great degree, the future of Pakistan depends on well-trained technicians.

Students take notes during a class held at the Lyallpur Agricultural University's new conservatory in Pakistan.

A Youth Club boy in the village of Gari Amir Khan, near Peshawar, concentrates on his task of braiding grass into stout rope.

A primary school teacher in the Gandaria District, Dacca, conducts a reading class in the courtyard, because of overcrowded conditions in the school.

Women students at the School of Fine Arts, Lahore, compose type as part of practical training in printing processes. In the last decade, women have been encouraged to take their place beside men in the world of business.

some manual work every week under the direct supervision of his teachers.

Efforts made to encourage education and to wipe out illiteracy are already bearing fruit. In 1970, some 7,000,000 children were in primary schools, more than double the number enrolled in schools in 1955. During the period 1960–66, an average of 2,700 new primary schools were opened each year; at present about 4,000 new primary schools are going up annually. Despite this pace, overcrowded classrooms and a critical shortage of qualified teachers remain as problems.

At the higher level, Pakistan now has 13 universities, as compared to only three at the time of partition. An average of 23,000 young men and women take their degrees each year.

At Punjab University in Lahore, a typing class is in progress.

A typical street in a small rural village of Pakistan has a bazaar which offers everything from homespun wools and fresh fruit to such popular Western products as Coca-Cola and Schweppes, served very warm.

FOOD

Pakistani cuisine, although basically spicy and fiery, is known for its richness and inventiveness. Some of the more popular dishes include *pulaos* (specially cooked meat and rice), *kofta* (meat balls), *murgh-i-mussalam* (stuffed fried chicken), and *shahi tukra* (sweetbreads cooked in milk and honey). The Pakistani equivalent of the Western hamburger is *chapli kebab,* patties of ground lamb mixed with green onions, dried pomegranate seed, and salt; these fried meat cakes are available everywhere from street vendors, who serve them with *nan,* a tough, leathery disc of slightly leavened bread. For those with a sweet tooth, there are *zarda,* made with sweet rice, nuts, and spices; *khorma,* made of tiny spaghetti, sugar, and small nuts; and *halva,* made of ground carrots, sugar, nuts and spices.

Pakistan is not a country of frozen and packaged foods as can be seen from this display of fresh fruit and olives in a typical rural market.

46

Sitting on a "charpoy," or rope bed, a young girl prepares food on the porch of her mud hut in a desert village near Peshawar.

A vendor in a village bazaar prepares pots of hot tea. Pakistan and Bangladesh are among the great tea-drinking nations of the world. Bangladesh produces over 60,000,000 pounds of tea a year.

A substantial luncheon is served to children in the Day Care Centre in Mohammedpur (an industrial area of Dacca). A training ground for social welfare students from the College of Social Welfare and Research, the Centre cares for 50 young children while their mothers are doing domestic work.

As in many other nations, wheat is the staff of life in Pakistan. *Chapatties*—flat wheels of unleavened bread tasting faintly of whole wheat—form the basis of every meal in Pakistan. In poor households, the chapatti is often the entire meal, with any other food spread thinly over the bread like butter.

Most Pakistanis outside of the large cities cook their food out-of-doors in small, clay, wood-burning stoves called *chulas* which rest on the ground. City dwellers have a larger version of the chula, usually as high as a table, resting on the floor of the kitchen, with a flue to carry the smoke out-of-doors.

Rice is the staple food for Bengalis. Here, in a village near Dacca, a woman prepares the evening meal, "puffing" the rice in a heated earthenware pot.

From the time of Pakistan's partition, women pitched in to help build their nation and they still form the country's cheapest worker force, especially in the monumental task of constructing link canals. These women transport bricks at the Sidhnai-Mailsi link canal which connects the Ravi and Sutlej Rivers.

5. THE ECONOMY

AT THE TIME OF PARTITION, Pakistan's economy was almost exclusively agricultural. There were no large industries, no native banks, few commercial enterprises and, almost no trained technicians, professional people, or skilled workers.

Since partition, considerable progress has been made in developing the country's relatively backward economy. New banks and businesses have sprung up, and an impressive amount of industrialization has occurred, with a strong development of technical, professional, and industrial skills.

Pakistan's economic development has been carried out under three five-year plans, the third of which went into effect July 1, 1965. The goal of the third five-year plan was to increase agricultural and industrial production by 40 per cent by 1970. More development funds than ever before were allocated to East Pakistan, partly to assuage that province's resentful feeling. A little more than half of the necessary expenditures were financed out of Pakistan's own resources. The balance came from external sources, including grants, loans and foreign private investment. Since 1947, Pakistan has had to rely heavily on economic assistance from a number of western countries —the United States, Great Britain, Australia,

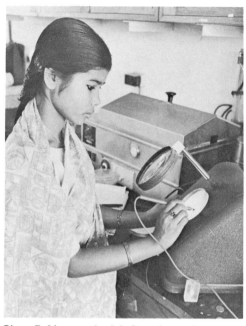

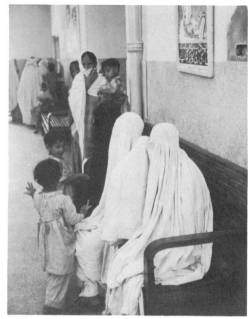

Since Pakistan gained independence, its women-folk have entered most of the professions with conspicuous success. Here a laboratory technician in the Cholera Research Centre in Dacca makes a culture count with an electronic counter.

Patients wait at the tuberculosis clinic in Rawalpindi which was established in 1961 with the technical assistance of UNICEF and WHO. During a two-year period, nearly one-third of the people examined at the clinic were found to be suffering from tuberculosis.

New Zealand, Canada, Japan, West Germany, France, and Italy. The World Bank and its affiliates, the International Development Association (IDA), and the International Finance Corporation (IFC), have invested heavily in productive projects in vital sectors of the country's economy.

By 1970, the goal of the third five-year plan

A technician seals bottles of saline solution used in the treatment of cholera.

Pakistani workmen lay brick paving along part of the Balloki-Suleimanke Link Canal in the Indus Basin.

seemed hopelessly out of reach, due mainly to barely keeping pace with the annual rise in population. The standard of living is still very low and the per capita income is one of the lowest in the world. Poverty and under-the skittishness of foreign and domestic

private capital. Current production seems to be employment are widespread among the masses of the population.

The economy, like much of everything else in Pakistan, has not yet fully recovered from the loss of Bangladesh, nor even the 1965 war with India over the disputed State of Kashmir when the United States cut off all economic and military assistance. In addition, Pakistan's meagre foreign-exchange reserves were further reduced by two subsequent years of drought that cut the agricultural output, forcing Pakistan to purchase more food from abroad. The United States resumed economic aid in the spring of 1966 and renewed limited military assistance in April, 1967. But, by December 1967, Pakistan's foreign currency reserves were 40 per cent below the 1966 level. Prices during this same period rose sharply, an alarming climb of 14 per cent in 1967 alone.

A workman with a goatskin water carrier washes part of the concrete superstructure of the almost completed Ravi Bridge at Lahore. The four-lane toll bridge, built with funds from an International Development Association credit to Pakistan, is an important link in the projected national highway from Karachi to Peshawar.

51

A group of trainees from the Technical Training Centre in Lahore visit the Pakistani Diesel Repair Shop while on a field trip to Karachi. The Centre, which was established with the aid of the United Nations Technical Assistance Administration, provides facilities for training students from Asian countries in advanced techniques of railway operating and signalling.

The immediate prospects for short-term improvement in the future economy are fairly good, thanks to the promise of bountiful wheat and rice crops. But the nagging problems of an increasing burden of debt and a critical shortage of managerial skills required to advance industry continue to cloud the long-term economic picture.

The pedicab, or bicycle rickshaw, is a common form of transportation in Bangladesh.

Porters unload bales of "pucca" (better quality) jute from sampans to take to the baling company in Dacca for processing.

AGRICULTURE

With about 75 per cent of its total working force engaged in agriculture, and more than 80 per cent of the population classified as rural, Pakistan's economy today, as before 1947, is still basically agricultural. Agriculture accounts for slightly less than half of the total national output, and agricultural products normally account for more than 50 per cent of Pakistan's total export earnings.

Jute, an annual tropical plant that is grown for the tough fibrous layer which lies between the outer bark and the central wood, grows well in the wet, alluvial soil of Bangladesh. The country produces over 70 per cent of the world's jute crop—5,000,000 to 6,000,000 bales annually. Mixed with silk, flax, and other

This typical farm is in the Chittagong Hill Tracts, a 5,600-square-mile area of hills and jungles, intersected by a network of winding rivers.

53

A bicycle and horse-drawn cart make their way across a field of Mexican wheat. This is a new variety, introduced into Pakistan through the efforts of United States agricultural technicians, and it has greatly increased the total wheat yield.

materials, jute is used in the production of burlap, cable, twine, oakum, paper, webbing, and backing yarns for linoleum and carpets. Cotton and cotton textile production now meets most of the country's needs and constitute the second largest export.

FOOD CROPS

The principal food crops are wheat and rice, the two critical items in Pakistan's grim race with famine in the face of an exploding population. To find the key to the onrushing food crisis, extensive experiments were conducted in

Sugar cane is loaded on a tractor in the Thall area of Pakistan. Pakistan produces over 28,000,000 tons of sugar cane a year, more than double the production of a decade ago.

Rice is still harvested by age-old hand methods in most of Bangladesh, with men using primitive cutting tools while women do the binding.

At the Bangladesh Textile Institute in Dacca, young apprentices receive practical training in jute weaving on a loom.

This old Bengali farmer is one of many benefitting from the improved irrigation and drainage system under construction in areas drained by the Ganges-Kobadak Rivers.

Water is raised from a well by an ancient device known as the Persian wheel. The wheel is usually turned by a blindfolded camel or bullock walking round and round in a circle. There are approximately 200,000 Persian wheels in operation in Pakistan.

1967 at the Pakistan Agricultural University and the Ayub Agricultural Research Institute near Lyallpur. The experiments with Mexican dwarf wheat proved that Pakistani farmers can more than double the production of any field in a season, just by sowing the Mexican wheat instead of conventional varieties.

OTHER CROPS

Other important commercial crops are tea, sugar, tobacco, and oil seeds. Cultivation methods, especially in Pakistan, are still generally primitive and the majority of rural people are subsistence farmers, who raise their crops only to live on, not to sell. Yields are low, and the output from year to year is dependent largely on the weather. In Pakistan sub-

In a village near Lahore, a modern tube well, run by electric power, provides the villagers with a plentiful supply of clear, fresh water for irrigation, drinking, or getting the Monday wash done.

With a humid climate and sloping hills, Sylhet, Bangladesh, is the main tea-producing area. In one of the 132 tea gardens of the District, Hindu women move as swiftly as grasshoppers as they pluck tea flushes (the tender bud and the top two leaves). It takes over 3,500 flushes to make a pound of processed tea.

stantial amounts of productive land have been lost through deterioration caused by salt deposits and waterlogging. In East Pakistan catastrophic floods and cyclones occur almost annually.

Attempting to control the monsoon floods is beyond the power of the government since 90 per cent of the catchment basin where flood control would be most effective lies in China, India, Tibet, and Nepal. In an effort to shore up the fertile Ganges River delta against the intrusions of sea water, 2,600 miles of dykes extending across Bangladesh's southern coast from the India border on the west to a point about 50 miles south of Chittagong are

A farmer winnows wheat at Salidagh, a village in Bangladesh. He wears a "lungi," a rectangle of tartan cotton, usually worn by Bengali Moslem workers.

Sampans line a quiet backwater in Bangladesh.

In a small rural village in Pakistan, a woman works a machine for cutting fodder.

currently under construction. Financed with the aid of a large loan from the United States Agency for International Development, the project will raise the productivity on 2,700,000 acres of land once the salinity in the protected soil is sufficiently reduced.

This plant at Lahore produces a wide variety of printed boxes and containers. Here a workman sends a board into a modern printing press.

Boatmen ply a tributary of the Ganges at Dacca, Bangladesh, in the same manner and in the same type of boats they have used for centuries.

INDUSTRY

Pakistan's industrial sector—manufacturing and mining but excluding power—now represents about 15 per cent of the country's activity. The manufacture of cotton textiles is the largest industry, employing about 200,000 workers in 120 mills. Current annual production of yarn is in the order of 520,000,000 pounds, and yardage of cloth is about 760,000,000. The jute mills of Bangladesh produce about 350,000 tons each year, the

New dockside cranes at the Port of Karachi, Pakistan's main gateway to the world, are part of a rehabilitation and modernization scheme carried out with the aid of two World Bank loans.

59

The trains of Pakistan have been modernized with foreign aid. Much old equipment remains, such as the second-class car which these people are boarding in the main station at Lahore. The development of road, rail, air, and river communications has contributed much to the successful growth of tourism in Pakistan.

bulk being exported; by 1970, jute manufacturers reported that their volume of production was more than double.

CHEMICALS

In the field of fertilizers—indispensable to a country where agriculture plays so important a

Karachi boasts that it has the finest airport in Asia. The country's national airline, PIA (Pakistan International Airlines) operates domestic and international services, including jet flights.

River boats line up along the busy waterfront of Dacca.

part—Pakistan produces about 350,000 tons of ammonia-based fertilizers using its own natural gas, limestone and gypsum as well as about

18,000 tons of superphosphate. Fertilizer production is expected to reach a million tons within the next few years. Pakistan is also a big producer of penicillin and other medical compounds, including santonin from its own crop of artemisia.

There are a number of publicly-operated enterprises in Pakistan, chiefly those for which private investment funds are not available. The Ayub administration, however, has placed major emphasis on private enterprise in

The Mangla Dam in Pakistan is the world's largest earth-filled dam. Under the terms of the Indus Waters Treaty of 1960, Pakistan is to construct a system of dams, link canals, and barrages to replace the irrigation water formerly used by India. The settlement allocated the waters of the Indus Basin's three western rivers—the Indus, the Chenab, and the Jhelum—to Pakistan and the waters of three eastern rivers to India.

61

At the Bangladesh port of Narayanganj, sampans carry cargo from ocean-going freighters to the river dock to unload.

Sailing boats ply the calm waters of the Meghna River in Bangladesh.

The railway station in Lahore is one of the many Western-style buildings in Pakistan which serve as reminders of British rule.

At Dacca, workers are busy constructing river traffic signs from galvanized iron, to replace old ones made from bamboo. Improved inland water transport is a vital matter on Bangladesh's great network of rivers.

Houseboats, including many operated by the Department of Tourism, cruise the many rivers and lakes of Bangladesh.

its industrial development policy. In both the private and public sectors, the goverment's principal goal is to reduce the country's dependence on foreign imports—raw materials or manufactured goods, mostly. A notably successful project is the Karachi Shipyard, which first went into production in 1956. This very well equipped installation not only builds vessels of all types but also executes ship repairs of all kinds. In line with the current policy of giving priority to heavy industry, two steel mills have gone into production—one in Chittagong, Bangladesh, the other at Kalabagh, Pakistan. Work is also well advanced for industrial complexes to produce machine tools, heavy electrical equipment, heavy forgings and castings.

Pakistan's industrial development is handicapped by the scarcity of minerals, a lack of markets, and low productivity by manpower.

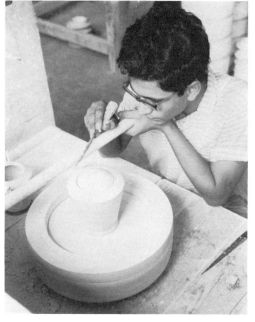

This artisan is at work in the moulding and casting section of a ceramics plant at Karachi.

INDEX